Selected Poems

BOOKS BY LEE GERLACH

Walking the Shore

Christmas Years

Placing the Past

Highwater

Ghazals

Sins of Old Age

Selected Poems

LEE GERLACH

Afterword by Harry Thomas

Swallow Press / Ohio University Press

Athens

Swallow Press / Ohio University Press, Athens, Ohio 45701
www.ohio.edu/oupress

Swallow Press / Ohio University Press books are printed
on acid-free paper ∞ ™

14 13 12 11 10 09 08 07 06 05   5 4 3 2 1

Jacket/cover art: *Morning Walk along the Thames, Port Meadow, Oxford*,
oil on canvas, by Christopher S. Gerlach

Library of Congress Cataloging-in-Publication Data
Gerlach, Lee.
  [Poems. Selections]
  Selected poems / Lee Gerlach ; afterword by Harry Thomas.
    p. cm.
  ISBN 0-8040-1081-1 (cloth : acid-free paper) — ISBN 0-8040-1082-X
(pbk. : acid-free paper)
  I. Title.
PS3513.E8648A6 2006
811'.54—dc22

                              2005022196

Contents

The Shepherd   1

Tabor Academy December   2

The Nightwalker   3

Stillness   4

In the Nightstruck House   5

The Last Novel   6

The Pilot's Walk   8

Lake De Noon   10

Genesis   11

The Vacationer   13

Early Morning in a Sierra Meadow   14

February Noon   15

White Nights in Mission Hills   17

Today I Heard the Late Hermit Thrush   20

Wakemanship   22

On Leave: 1943   24

January, 1980: Near Port Meadow   25

Sharp's Oxford, #1 Farndon Road   27

Molior Comes Home   29

Molior to His First Wife   31

Talking of Molior   33

Hermetic V: "She stood at the window looking away
    and down"   35

Hermetic VII: "She had heard of the country of the mind"   37

Hermetic XI: "Someday they will live here in this house" 38

The Old Poet at Full Moon 39

Legends 41

Some Years After 47

Adam 49

After a Long Illness 51

The Birds of Egypt 53

Kung Li Writes to His Father 56

Psyche 58

Walking the Shore Thinking of Su-Shih 59

Wally in the Park 61

Willowrun 65

When I Came to Cerillos and Mádrid, New Mexico 67

Lake Nine 74

Sister Theophila at Fond du Lac 76

Galisteo, New Mexico 78

Later 80

An Oxford Winter 82

Dear Tsvetaeva 93

Walking in Snow at Midnight 95

So Why? 96

Autumn Wind 98

Yes, 100

Afterword by Harry Thomas 103

The Shepherd

Stranger—Believe me.
Clear, clear nights for many days then,
too clear, haunting, for comfort.
The sheep were restless,
astray, and we little better.
It was as though heaven had opened,
swallowed the moon, and the silence
became wide and widening without end,
and the land, the small grass turned silver,
and the familiar avalanche of stars
retreated, leaving but one,
one in the wrong place, too brilliant
to gaze long at. So it was.

An omen? We are too used to them,
forewarned by the wizards and soothsayers.
Yet, something was going wrong.
We could feel it in the absence
of darkness in our souls,
and sense that something was coming.

Tabor Academy December

New England is deserted:
a salt-pale beach somewhere
near Mattapoisett.

The tired headmaster
crosses the soccer field
thinking of his youth,

the days mastering Schumann,
the stolen adumbration
unnoticed when he plays.

Paper trapped in the alder thick
and white houses beyond
perched on granite blocks.

There is a tease in the trees.
A veil of twigs and branches,
a cloudline of wood

where the sun darkens, heavy
with patience, a mouth
perfectly silent.

Sippican opens and closes
quietly under the dock
like a hissed confession.

The Nightwalker

Soul of a mission, troubling, you feel
The icy darkness mounding the old houses.
Their storm windows glitter like welled steel.
Walking the street, you start as a door closes.

An old man in a robe stands on his porch
In the thin snow. He looks out to listen
For what may be wandering there in mean March
Unwilling to be known, and, seen, you hasten—

The unknown one, the dark, muffled stranger—
Through his mystery. Something has taken his life,
A late snow fluttering, leaving only the anger
Of age and ageless remorse seeking relief.

And he must watch you fling by unaccosted
Over only a scuffed trace in the white—
Imprint and answer, an enigma wasted
Upon despair, yet one clued of the night.

Stillness

He paused where a bronze and brown fritillary hung,
Sipping on milkweed. The eyes on its wings closed
As it gathered them together to become a leaf.

They had come upon each other as in a dream
Where two wisdoms meet, each testing the other.
There was a slight breeze and the stiff leaf tipped.

He was sure. It was a small pleasure to be ancient
And unforseen in a simple wilderness,
Not least of all to remain silent and wait.

Who would move first? Who prove the other right?
Could they, would they stay there poised forever,
The sun stop, the rain never fall?

Surely, he knew? Yes. And moving on,
He watched the leaf dither away and fall
Into its future of thoughtless salvaging.

"This," he said, "riddle me though it may,
Has no meaning. Only the pause makes sense,
Only the silence between this and that."

And, walking slowly, threading among the rocks,
He carried within him the fragile butterfly
As one bearing a drop of water to the Lord of Hosts.

In the Nightstruck House

Here in my arms I carry you
As one day you may carry me.
You will not wake to what I do.
The house is black without degree.

I hold you thus, the only cause
Worth mentioning of all I know.
It does not move by any laws;
Mover itself, yet it may go.

Perhaps I hold you then for this:
I may not hold you long nor well,
For as you stir you change, and kiss
Nor cry may overmuch compel.

Small boy, small boy, I give you back
To the warm groaning of your bed,
And sighing sleep, and gentle wrack
Of time converging on your head.

The Last Novel

Even the long gray days and wild swept flaws
Of rain beating the trees down seemed kind.
No one dropped by. No one troubled to write.

He rose earlier, the dark, a new companion
Whose endless images were filled with voices,
Whose casual gestures promised and denied.

He thought to give them names, eyes and faces
They could have lived as their own. They met, he knew,
In an English garden, in a maze of tall boxwood.

How often he has seen them there, embraced,
And, as the plot would have it, how lost they were,
And rescued, unwilling to confess their truths.

Well, that would never do. It is raining harder.
The mystery, if there was one, solves itself
Like weather in which the sun makes a mistake.

He stood, mindless, at the great high window
Listening to fragments of conversation
That lay in another world on the table behind him.

They were leaning at dusk on a balustrade
Overlooking the Grand Canal. The years later,
The unwritten letters fed their indirections.

They had been too young to believe they were,
Too intelligent in a mild-mannered way
To resist invitations of a long grieving.

Now their gentle, kind loneliness took heart
From the still expanse of water. When they turned
Back to the salon, their author wept for them.

The Pilot's Walk

We can go on a hundred years
Like this, admiring simple things
In their setting—what belongs
And what does not, as each appears:

What in the thicket hangs beside
The wild berry, an orange leaf,
And what below the olive roof,
Raw beams where dusty spiders stride.

Painted girls in the old houses
Leaning from windows on the walk.
Harsh voices. Voices that, singing, speak.
Lank horses in loose and scarred harness.

Regret in parting, confused, still.
Meeting that promises regret.
Black hair tumbling its full weight.
Night's weight tangled with the hill.

Dead men thrown in the woods all week.
Helmets and belts that catch the sun.
Vermillion pools, earthworks, wine
Left standing. Branches and birds that creak.

Like this, admiring, vision clears.
The pastoral efficiency
Of mind turns up what it can see,
And wanders on a hundred years.

Lake De Noon

Sunk to the oarlocks a green boat
hangs in the clear water. Hardly a ripple,
not one breath of cool air all day long,
and I sit reading Darwin on the porch.
Look up, across the lake. Even flies rest.
Waiting for the last summer of the thirties to end.
Bluegill and sunfish lie in the sandy shallows,
breathing among the motionless, dark reeds.

Genesis

The place to begin is a desert.
Darkness lies upon it full length,
and a cold wind struggles through cholla,
creosote bush, and white, laid grass.
In the dead-end, lateral canyons,
the old palms tremble and thrash.
Loose, rotting stone slides and drops.

Under the smother, horned toads, iguanas,
speckled rattlers, and kangaroo rats
stir in the great Self, and he wakes.
The earth is moved, tracked by their lives.
A reverberation checks in the grasses
and settles in sandy swales. A light,
promising its harsh way, basks in the East.

I sit up in my mummy-bag. Shall I not
claim a victory over such solitude?
Lying here all night, unable to sleep,
I have run upon many things, all of them
my only life: peopled, emptied, true
and untrue, imagined, possible and not,
and through it all, the hard, uneven ground.

By the hour harder, fretted with pebbles
whose ambition to bruise I here attest,

the dry earth becomes a paradigm of the real.
It is unshakeable, yet shakes. It is hard
and a dense solid, yet some of it I move
with the pad of one finger. It is deserted,
and it is surely the right place to begin.

The Vacationer

I am tired, and everything is an effort:
looking at the hills, reading your letter,
drinking the cold coffee. I say I know
the cause—there is too much to resist.

One guards still an immense simplicity,
unwilling to admit. One gazes from the rampart
out across the river sparkling in the sun.
The hills slide up under the dark trees.

Something gathers there. You can almost hear
the sound of a dry wheel turning, dragged
in the dense grass, crushed violets, clover.
Yet, nothing is there; the resistance a yearning.

There is only the day coming in force.
Your long-awaited words come on the light,
but, even assenting, I do not understand
what you say. It is like reading the trees.

Passivity and a civil disquiet, I fast,
perfectly willing to let things be
just as they are. Yet I fear that I
am but tricked to weariness and guard that best.

Early Morning in a Sierra Meadow

There were deer straying, shoulder deep
In the low haze, over the water-sweet grass
Of the meadow, moving across banded rivulets,
Steely water, and among pale cropping stone.

There were birds, shadows of birds, and their echoes
Drifting in early aspens and blue spruce.
The gray mountain rose quickly to bitter pine.
There were clouds, winds. There was the scent of sleep.

Granite and reed mace framed the glacial lake,
A black mirror, pure surface ringing with quiet.
There were numberless particles of time
And air, suspended, turning to color, light.

Yet there was nothing. The deer, startled, turned
To brush that was air as the grass and the veiled spruce.
Meadow and man, inconstant, leaned toward noon,
And the blue shadows shortened over the ground.

February Noon

Tomorrow it will be
    six days
        since she died.

Today it is five
    and you could not tell
        by the weather.

The sick orange tree
    trimmed to the bone
        is in full flower.

The sky is empty
    neither coming nor going
        in any direction.

You would think
    something would act
        a little different.

You would like to
    believe something
        but what?

You know already
        the solemn tone
                in Saint Vincent's.

It will be hot, stifling
        and the parochial windows
                will yellow everyone.

Yes. You will go.
        It is right. It
                is something to do.

Yesterday it was four days
        and the day before three
                and the day before two.

And many days before
        we sat in such a sun
                with the children.

White Nights in Mission Hills

1.

Night of a full, bleak moon. I wander out
Under the heavy trees, layered with light,
Through a whirr of shadows. Rough black grass,
And grass dyed lunar white, and pine and skunk
Staining, whetting the air's pale edge. Think,
What deep relief brings the day down to this.
Changing all change, the glaze darkening
Blurs feral October's end. And still your face
Hovering where I look. I know you bring
Me, chastened, back from the shadow's wavered cut,
But still the great drift, error, draws me out
To want to be lost. Groping, I touch the string,
Tethered by what I am and you are not.

2.

The city darkens, sinking past midnight,
And the valley freeway stirs faintly, exhausted.
Standing at the screen door, I watch the wind
Struggle through the grass. Tomorrow we mow,
And all those creatures, seething to rise,
Dithering toward mortality, must perish.
But here, leaping from darkness the wind
Is my childhood; the rich scent of standing hay,
Alfalfa in the hill-field and crickets bleating.
I am overwhelmed. How I prayed to be perfect
And permanent there! I was the morning, the field,
The hushing sun adrift on bearded grass.
Everything is in place to the last tree:
The broken harrow beside the barn, the mouse
In the mealy seed-loft, the dung-green stalls,
Rime on the hayfork and a fair winter morning.
The cows blow and clatter in the racks. And
When everyone else lies asleep, the clock groans
And the squat kitchen pump wheezes softly.
Moonlight pools on the floor, shifts like water.
And summer: driving to pasture in the cool woods.
The path dips below the mossy granite outcrop,
The cattle, dawdling, hook at the mounded brush.
The slow spring drips from a flaw, pigweed,
Tall ferns and fiery nettles, then, opening to the shore,
On the pale sand over mica a small, sudsy surf,
How the blue light dazzles! Whitefish Bay,
I dream and loiter, looking toward Beaver Island.

3.

In the deep ravine that spills out to the valley,
Furtive among the black mounds of laurel,
The white doe wanders. More than once, startled,
I have come upon her at twilight or at dawn
Browsing among the flowerbeds, and her light thudding
Cups on the air, her scut bobs as she swings
Down into the brush. This is no forest retreat,
No Syrinx lounges in a covert here. Dry country,
Surrounded by city, this archaic place resists
Tomorrow. The owl hunts here. Kit fox and possum
And skunk clamber through cover up to the lawns.
Children of moonwalkers watch from the dark door.
Here they come, shadows emerging from black ice,
Old fleece, a blur, a soft bristle sliding.
Hesitant, they gather at the edge of the clipped yard,
Stand there, alert and ancestral, waiting to speak.

Today I Heard the Late Hermit Thrush

I miss the life I live.
New living wears a hard,
Impatient stare. I starve
In eating what I've hid.

I cannot look aside.
I cannot wait to grieve.
Old passions still recede.
Strange hungers still arrive.

My body wears me well,
Its thoughtlessness a bait
Or, fulling like a sail,
A promise and a threat.

My mind, my reprobate,
Whose syllogisms lie
And prove me ever right,
Trusts in another day.

And, Oh, my heart, my friend,
How listless you have grown.
Is it that all you've been
Resigns to be a sound

Remembered like the thrush
At dusk when the sun sets
And all that once was fresh,
Wet blue ravels and rusts?

Well, well, we come and go,
Heart, body, mind and all
We've hoped to be a soul.
In the blind dark they call,

And what they summon wakes
To gaze across the room,
Sweeping the thousand books
In which they penned its name.

Wakemanship

The great gold carp bend
and feather in the half-light.
Each opens like a mailed gate,
and night comes to an end.

Someone has covered my eyes
with earth. The weight
is unbelievable; moist
and cool enough to please

any slug abed. How sweet
life seems at ten
in the morning when
privilege masks light

and I awake deep in sleep,
refusing to move.
Come, someone I love!
Reality will keep

blossoming, take leaf,
no matter how
we rest or go.
Now darkness, like a reef,

building below the surf,
eternity, sighs
and my mind lies
in an arm's coral curve.

On Leave: 1943

He had given up on a necessary faith,
Including himself, born to believe,
To know the truth a living thing.

Now in England in winter, he had lost
Even the sun. "Heigh Ho, the Wind and the Rain!"
And a war to believe in, die for.

He was cold, cold, never to be warm again.
That morning a dripping mist, grey, leaching,
Yet trees along the lane were beautiful.

They knew, never heart heavy as lead
Thudding, water in grass falling from the eaves
And monotony the splendor.

Empty the small, parish church, Saint Margaret's,
A lovely place to sit and taste loneliness,
Unforgiven, resolute, mournful, comforted.

He knew the war would end. He would stand
Knee deep in the Pacific surf, watch the sun
Repeat its ember faith, sinking into the horizon.

January, 1980: Near Port Meadow

Oxford sick with the sickness
of scholars coughing in the street,
and I was bushed and fagged
and, as Gerard would say, fashed
like silt-sallowed withes tugged
along the sleek, slewed riverbank.

Here, too, a century ago,
he had leaned and looked down
from the brick-work bridge
examining his weary despair,
wearier for its wantonness
and that he could want it
and not, not want to escape
self-hood's sour brutality,
the night rustling down
through sad, clubbed willows
and up from the hissing stream.

Where next? What next
when the body becomes colder
than spitting mist, and mind,
rounding itself, comes upon
a blank meditation humming
like black water, a before

and after without memory
whose sunlit meadows, high clouds,
Ribblesdale from the Fells,
hare-bell and primrose, fields purple,
struck up from brush and broom
will remain civil in wilderness
for other eyes to remember
and write down to save?

Perhaps he knew perhaps,
the Soul's wisdom rivering away,
heavy with darkness or, cobalt-carried,
a deepening sky, a new skydom
flooded with ambers and golds.

I take him up again in a book.
It is night. He writes Bridges
about Pindar, Greek meters.
He is sick, dying in Dublin
at the end of the world, lost,
his poverty unanswerable.
We lean on the crowned bridge
and, shoulder to shoulder silence,
gaze at the swift, swept water.

Sharp's Oxford, #1 Farndon Road

The interior was severe, bland and cold,
and common English, some pictures,
etchings dim under dusty glass
like sudden intrusions in a grave memory
always somewhat askew.
The walls in their sullen hostility
had an uncertain, greenish cast,
and the doors with their high-set knobs
and deep key-holes seemed arresting so that
to come or go assigned a conclusion.

The bookcases were hip-high
filled with the read and reread
memorials of a distant future
which, like a reviewed necessity,
preserved a demand
and a power, no matter why neglected,
yet articulate as brittle, foxed pages
and the community of dead poets
enduring for awhile a just penalty.

Ten years of that winter solitude
became one more day of shadowless
blurred irreverance. I walked there,
stood there, ready to understand,

to regret the uselessness of regret
for desires and unrequitable devotions
so much like my own. I had come back
into my own future to be bemused,
once more to send a letter
I would never write to myself,
because him I wrote to had casually
moved away and left no return address,
like Sharp's friend, Edward Thomas.

Molior Comes Home

There were unpossessed fragments here and there,
A tuft of rope bedded in bark, the square for herbs
One solid wig of crab-grass, emerald green.

The old oaks seemed no larger, the sun the same,
The dry, peppery scent of youth confirmed
By his abandoning, the setting free.

He had not been young here, yet even then
He had not been theirs in a plain, usual way.
They saw it in his pale gray eyes and dry face.

Now, small as then, a forked-stick wandering out
Across the stubblefield in the white moon
Of October, he still cast the shadow they prayed

Would not be lost, caught in its grave slumber.
He paused to look back down where the house heaved
Its eyes, moon-struck, against the Hallow's night.

For him, it was like a mockery of noon
Rejoicing, a *Ludi Saeculares*
In whose choral andante the dead prevailed.

They had remembered him as someone met
And lost in a place made foreign by his coming—
And all their labor mindlessness as grace.

He felt their pity, their love and hurt restraint
Tremble about him—sonorous music, a coda
That recedes and fades, adrift in a silenced voice.

And yet this, too, spoke wisdom's muttered place
In which his soul knelt down to clutch its dust
And raised it to the moon and let it go.

Molior to His First Wife

My Dear:
      I write wondering where you are.
Forty-five years of silence and cold truth,
Both envious, both obsolete as youth
Grow parsimonious, seen afar.
I cannot think you have not thought of me
As someone foreign like yourself, abroad
In familiarities unfamiliar, half-awed,
Half-wretched, weak, leaning the rail at sea.

Today, that sickness surfs among my trees
And draws back, tearing at the shore.
We are both Westward now, and the wind's roar
Merely imagination, merely a breeze.
Time in my garden entertains your face
Among azaleas. How beautiful you were,
I feel but cannot see and now endure
Your meaningless visitation in this place.

You did not come, I know, because I called.
It was not like you then. It can't be now.
And could you speak your voice would not endow
My presence here with yours, again appalled
That we had lived for love without a thought,
Mindless in celebration of desires

We worshipped, our bodies like twin, altar fires,
Our promises the incense of an ought.

Yet here you are once more, untouched by life,
Neither my own nor yours. Your endless cares,
Your wrinkled throat, your happinesses, fears
Have never come to pass. Woman and wife,
You move about the room. The Florida light
Streams on the ceiling. Cars pass in the street
Below under the tall palms. We meet
In wartime, stroll, pluck hibiscus at night.

Talking of Molior

Time and again he'd said the numberless things,
Their shapes, their colors, their places were one—
That blue was green, the mountains waves, the hero
Some simple man reading late at night
In an old house, a ruin before he was born.

We spoke of this, she and I, sitting in the dark
On the cottage porch. The lake contained a moon.
Pines on the island loomed black, a bright black,
And an intimate fire gleamed on the north shore.
We were repeating the end of summer and thinking

As he had thought there, grown old and patient.
We heard his voice in our words, the long pauses,
Slow sentences hanging, drifting aside, the tremble
And sudden animation that made his life ours.
It was as though he had known we would come back,
That what he had made possible would take place.

She said, "Do you think he knows what none can know
Without breath and failure? Because you sound
Like him, is his body telling us the way
That picnic fire streams across till water
Is the fire he muses among weary angels?"

"There are," I said, "times like this when he
Seems more alive, completing me, than I am
Myself, so that I wonder where his truths
Intend our ignorance to go? This hour,
More precious, deep as mixed comfort and desire

Must contain any eternity we dream,
No matter the loneliness it promises,
Nor want of peace, nor loss of speech, nor touch.
Belief has taught me nothing I believe
Beyond that small fire and the need for nothing more."

She put her glass down on the porch rail.
There was a fire in it and fires in her eyes
And among the motionless leaves. A new silence
Repeated itself lifting from the lake
And the pines became men eager for the moon.

Hermetic V

She stood at the window looking away and down
to the green valley through and beyond the trees:
They were real, and the sight of them,
half-visionary. The feel of them, their names
on her tongue: podocarpus, cypress, eucalyptus
and late jacaranda, now but promising
clouds of white to violet and purple blossoms,
wintered, waiting for the right season and
the wordless sentencing and again
Ceres' mythology explained.

All things in that grand display having their say
remain possible. The rose in the glass
opening day after day, revealing itself,
speaking to the closed books ranged on the wall . . .

O red rose! rose of the midnight's silence,
rose of the sun and heart-fareing,
caught in the crevices and revelations
in the mind, undulating beyond time!

Yet the more and more was there as well.
She stood hip deep among the white lilies
and the vision expanded beyond the small bed
beside the house, out and away:

a valley, a sea of lilies, their long, soft,
leathery leaves lolling like tongues, dewy and swayed
in the sexual ecstasy of green, green green.

Hermetic VII

She had heard of the country of the mind,
the dry hills of Plato, time-wearied the dialogues,
wave-tattered along the shore where West
is no longer a wonder but a sun burning out,
fuming into the sea.
It is hard to think of the day, a new space that opened
itself and came to itself, again realized
as a sun, a brandishing of thorns on a rose
and visionary Spring scheming without consciousness.

Just imagine, she mused, not as the last goddess left
at the banquet, the debate foundered, the goblets
tipped over staining the table red, but just herself—
just imagine a world in which all allusion was barred.
There where the kind, searching allegories
of reality were unforgivable, the last tale,
the last myth told.

The sea could not resemble. The rose she bent to
could not be like the evening sun
and her love could not flame. Nothing could be worth.
Would there not be (if it could be?) one thing only?
And what could that be?
Would it not be this, a rose whose scent
she could not say, indifferent?

Hermetic XI

Some day they will live here in this house,
those we never knew, those we never
invited in, and nothing will be the same.
They will lie in bed, wake, and listen to our rain
dripping slowly from the loquat tree near the window.
One night they will walk at midnight on the lawn,
listen to the mockingbird entertain
the full moon, his repertory more than imitations.
They will stroll under the trees we planted
sixty years ago, pleased by the dappled sun and shade.

And, she thought, raking the yellow leaves:
are we not the same?
We pause, as we must, almost transformed
by the wonder of these hyacinths, azaleas and roses.
How can one honor their silence,
endure their will to be beautiful?
How can one stay silent, knowing the language
of flowers could be our own—
we who have nothing?

She wanted to speak simply, to embrace
the syllables of youth and the wordless intonations
that had discovered her.

"These," she said, "are the gratitudes that own me."

The Old Poet at Full Moon

Bacchus, I know your fine transports
and dances with Thalia, know the promise,
sensual, forgettable.
I do not feel myself a ruin,
though it is true I've fallen down, lay there,
my pillars that held me up turned tumbrills
scattered along the hillside in harsh sun
mid ants, butterflies and dry weed, dead Acanthus,
and what's left of me, shadowed fluting.

Sitting on the ground, toasting the moon,
reciting a poem about Idea, about nothing
that could remember itself, yet able to remember,
life pleases the soft, comforting grass.

Friends, shadows of shades, be as you were,
still able and ambitious for love.
Absence is almost a clear confession,
carved in Greek, rain weathered, Time weathered,
word weathered.
Dear Venus, soften thy disdain.
Grant those who have known the virtue and ardor
of verse a fulfilling draught of rich Canary
that they may sing as once before.

Tonight, bless me, still the last of friends.
Icy goddess, what now would you have me do?
Let me see, and tomorrow I will start,
gather a pile of shards and raise a monument,
in it a secret chamber, and chiseled on its walls,
names of the serious souls, about them
a frieze, twined vines with laurel and bay leaves
and clusters of purple grapes in an iambic dance.

But wait . . . there must be painted there
gentle, musical harmonies,
flutes, tempered strings, violin, cello and bass.
Space well the chords and silences but never fail
to repeat the meaningful phrase.
Let the touch and go, the vibrating finger,
remain human and anonymous as the gods allow,
always in keeping, holding on.

Ah, Venus, you remain as Apollo and Hermes knew you,
far too brilliant, forever remote to be merely the moon,
and what of the stars that prick the darkness
in the cloistering hood of night?
Yet it is good to be alone now, the sole witness
in a self, favored and fooled.
Do you care? Do you recall last night, yourself,
or the silvered hill where the black cypresses
leaned against your breast?

Legends

For N. Scott Momaday, Kiowa

I.

When I traveled, I loved being on the way.
When I arrived, no matter where, I felt a fool.

On the train in winter, I wandered beyond myself,
Picked my way up the cuts in the river gorge,

Heard the thunder of the Yangtze mingling the Snake,
Saw the bleached bones of bison and men,

Filled my hands with snow and followed the deer—
High on the mountains, listened to the steady wind.

I kept wanting to get out and be left behind.
In Colorado, I tracked through deep drifts among spruce,

Came to a small, failed house, blackened by years.
The peeling wallpaper was filled with baskets of roses.

I sat there for miles of time and dropped my book,
No longer needed my ticket, nor food, nor sleep.

II.

In a silver-green meadow leveled by the river,
Year and again the Sac and the Fox have come.

There are things down in the ground, tricked in the trees
That have learned the resolute skill of water.

We know their names. They come to each of us
Without regard, Pinau and Pakitona.

Thunder and lightning play unabusive
As braves running stick and ball at La Crosse.

The grass is soft and sweet underfoot, and the day
Rose ready, full of our belief and witness.

We will invent peace, coursing the long field,
Speed home, catch a second breath and find it.

III.

The sun in white buckskin worked with beads
Walks the sky bearing a burning shield.

The earth is a color made for poets and children.
It is a thrill and flush, the power of ripening.

The great spruce tree knows. Its roots capture
The six springs. Its tip wavers the clouds.

Thunder is a bird whose wings flash the dark heavens
That zig-zag like the rivers, blanch the canyon walls.

I have been there. I have seen the files
Of feathered men pound the earth, dancing

To notify the underworld and all the ancestors
And dark Sipapu that the obligation is fulfilled.

I did not enter the secret cave in the mountainside
To realize the fiery afterward of deep snow.

IV.

I've spent weeks now running, running away.
I dodge and bend down like muskrat in the reeds.

The myrtles are in bloom. I shake them down,
Remember the taste of allspice and heady cloves.

Now it is ten years later, as it was then:
Rabbit-brush outlines, gold fields and acacias,

And Puyé, a cliff city girdled in the escarpment,
Ruins everywhere, past Otawi, past Tsankawi,

Past trails worn hip deep, past dancing places.
There the lizard runs and the magpie flies.

Everything is familiar as sun and moon
And hunger and satiety and desire to be older.

      * *

That land has many tongues, tall-topped potreros
Looking across the puma-blonde plain, hauntings—

Feathery pines and small creeks and clan signs cut
In canyon walls: Sun Clan, Snake Clan, and Lightning.

How often I have been there filled with the remorse
Of a late comer, wanting the moccasin's wisdom,

There to watch the year-long stream slip and veil
Over the basalt barrier of White Rock Canyon.

There is the unearthly-earthy beauty of less
As more, I could be content with bastions of stone.

Run, marsh-mind, run! Run lizard over
The ridges that held the sleeping mats in place.

V.

In spring flowers, such as those described,
The ovary is placed above the other parts.

Is that not like beginning at the cadenza?
The violins waiting, their pistils at ready?

Wildflowers in the freestanding woods, Wisconsin
Deepens, staminate—a green, left-handed mitten.

It seeks to compose the lake. It is Chippewa quiet.
Swept by the wind, it rattles seeds, mullein and rice.

Near La Crosse, the oak savanna meets hardwood.
Fox and Sac mingle drums in the night.

Wherever you go—the grass family, slender
And tall with hollow, round stems, spikelets, scales.

There the triticum ripen, the inner and outer sleeves,
Feathery stigmas savor the sun and are grain.

Here in the wooded uplands the buttercups flourish.
You will see them all along the roads, half-foreign.

I have gazed into the bristly crowfoot, its hairs
Spreading like the sun, and forgotten the way back.

I have walked these woods, have sucked the grass.
I have listened to the oaks, the andantes of waterleaf.

Some Years After

I did not think to try.
I gave you what I was,
Half-tempered in some lie
We live without its cause.

You seemed to understand.
Complexity bemused us.
You held me in your hand
And ruled what most confused us.

Our sons arrived and grew.
They trusted you to treasure
Futures they must do
To honor your firm measure.

Yet ease turned change, came true
Like arrows in their flying,
And I left to undo
The errors of your dying.

I loved you with my life,
Since it was all I had.
Now in those shapes of grief
And passions of the mad

I see myself revealed
And wonder at those years.
Who could believe, concealed,
Loving, I fed your fears?

Yet when you hover near
In the dark morning hours,
I wake, as once, to hear
You speaking to the flowers,

Iris and rose, aflame
In the half-light of distress,
And though I seem the same
What you are none can guess.

Adam

Until you brought her here there was nothing
To notice or desire but you beyond
All notice, forbidding desire not forbid,
Not even a cloud from whose bright, folding domes
A voice might come, for till she rose beside me
From the soft grass there was only loneliness.
It never occurred to me to mind it then.
And you, what then were you to me to want
Who wanted nothing? Was it in retrospect
You called it "Paradise"?
                                          I was content
In an emptiness like yours, saw without seeing
Birds in the trees, light shimmering on the pool,
Heard in the dawn wind sigh among the leaves,
Touched the cold stones, tasted the tart berries
That came to hand, and slept and waked refreshed
Needing nor sleep nor waking.
                                          I find it hard
To believe you could resent our equal state,
That our undying, cold tranquility
In which all things, oblivious as ourselves,
Remained unknowing, had to have an end.
I knew you as myself without a mind,
And till you made her, tore her from my side,
I lived without a thought. She it is made

My mind as she made love and made the trees
Where we could walk in sun and trembled shade.
You it was made her love's temptation here,
And, doing so, not only brought, not unforseen,
I now must think, love but the world as well.
For, loving her, I see, and hear, and touch
The substance of all being, and though we die
In mute obedience to your legal wiles,
I think at last and understand your error.

After a Long Illness

It is a small damage
the wind has made in the maples,
and though now they bleed
and their frayed sleeves flap
slowly in the morning breeze
they are well and but worn in
more securely to this place,
warped more cunningly into
the branching bouquet in air
time leaves in its long wake.

Thus it must be. Flowering
in space, shifting the light,
and the light grazing your eye,
an eye less able, simple of soul,
the small wheel spinning,
filling the spindle in your heart,
all this in a breath, all
this in the renewed awaking.

We are here once more, though
it seemed but a moment ago
that the storm could not end
and that everything had gone
and was surely going into the

insatiate purse: darkness,
but the frail nitre, supplication
and the fiery, damp offering
of the body, titled, grave, won
through in this loose daylight,
a fluttering reprieve.

"Yes, there's tea, if you wish,
And there's someone to see you."

The Birds of Egypt

At first they flaunt impossible reminders
of distances and the soul's impatience,
its desire for wings, the soft lift and waft
of the invisible rising and the sun's pressure,
level along every flared primary and covert.
But then a thousand years pass, and thousands more,
nestings brooded, clutches in tall marsh grass,
hectares of small bones sinking, breaking apart
in the alluvial drift, feathers drifted to the sea.
Egypt is but a beginning, and Asia, Americas,
islands scattered carelessly and tallest peaks
where eagles abrade the earth away, and palms
burst into flame, the Phoenix, ash-risen.

Like the mind alive with its prisoned hope,
they sweep about us, imaginable yet real,
hovering motionless against the clouds,
plunging into the green-blue swell of oceans,
flicking from twig to branch, untouching, untouched.
Their sweet clamors invade our dreams, their cries
through strangling mist at twilight, their brutal caws
over the battered corn-fields white with snow
become our own half-remembered, practiced
anticipations of what we are and must be.
In the loneliness of a long winter darkness,

we await their return, believe they will come
again to our trees, visionary, sure.

Surely, should admiration vanish away
forever and all the monuments sink down,
the last army perish and the last city
filter to the sea, they will be there
to write their wisdom in the river's mud.
This much an Amenhotep knew, his tomb
beatified with Ibis and the sun's Harrier.
This much his followers understood: the sky
is the sun's haven and every bird sun-sent,
an emissary secreting in its wings
the imponderable transformations of air
and light and earth's deep darkness, the deep sleep
that trembles, half-awake, and stays to dream.

There was more silence in it than we know,
and, pausing in the tombs among the rows
on rows of silent birds, Ibis and Hawk,
mummied as though eternity were but
another day to wander in, to fast,
to measure the sun's descent, to walk back
with a pious lowering of the head, to eat
ripe figs, drink sweet wine, to celebrate,
this must have been, those thoughtless years ago,
an overture to peace the dead must know.
Soft sandals stir the dust. Lamplight quivers.
No word can give this Hawk back to the sun
or flush this Ibis from the swaying reeds.

And yet, as one that comes from the bright sun
into an ancient darkness treasured here
by millions of treasured emblems of their life,
those with hooked claws and beaks, steady assassins,
and those content to pluck the Nile's new muck,
I feel the dark amazement of that world,
and blinded, hear the millions of bound wings
press against their cords, crackle to rise
as once they did when nothing saved them from death.
I feel the flap and glide, the silent stoop,
and high-pitched scream of quarry in the tomb,
and in the river valleys and marshes I lift
my frog-spawned, dripping head against the sun.

Kung Li Writes to His Father

You were sincere when you tried to write.
Some of the characters fooled you. Some came fresh
Out of the willow tatters in the river,
Some from the dry soil, cracked beneath your feet.
You had something in mind, an old, old mind
That was not a mind at all but an empty bowl.
Even when the long rains came, it held nothing
Sitting out there thinking to be full.
The heavens seeped away. The clay dried white.

Today I bought a silk farm, trays of cocoons,
Racks stacked to the roof with soft, white weavers.
Ten million million worms spin silver strands
In mindless preservation. Ten million trace
One character the moon slept upon
And woke to find repeated endlessly
In tight fish-scales, glitter in shallows fading,
Their supple carriers, side-up, round-eyes glazed.
How could a keeper of worms and stinking fish
Presume to think at all or dream to say
Or hope to write what centuries of life
And death have given us to know and save?

Father, I honor your innocence and faith.
I see them sitting with you on the steps,

The river singing its reeds, the late swallows
Crowding under the eaves and the moon rising.
I sit on the marble bench outside my house,
Troubled by troubles I do not deserve,
The ignorance of those, abused, I judge,
The arrogance of those I humbly serve.
I want only to write a poem in verse
Equal to a meaningless gesture, a hillside
Covered with succulent clover, the rape
Of wild raspberry, and the startled lark
Flinging me at the sun.
                              If in truth,
It turned out that you were the family poet
And I a pretender scrawled beneath your name,
No matter how elegantly—my learning merely
Scholarly, bent on obscurity, myself a note,
A paradox of devotions misunderstood,
I could rest content, for only the poem
Matters, the poet a silk-worm in the dark,
Anonymous, anonymous as words.

Psyche

Today, a sapphire dragonfly in the room,
A hovering blaze. Last night, a dream of death.
Both seemed simple assents perplexing life,
Filled with mixed impertinence and sense.
All comes and goes in an impelling balance
Of forms and fires beyond our best invention.
And, when we reflect, those small lights cast
Gleam and dissolve within us, clouds adrift.

We count on the wind. We meet and part
As promises and haunting invitations.
Should I conceive a firmer, finer phrase:
One in which all my tedium stood apart
And I, among things vacant as blind glass,
Blurred to a mist, a whiteness changing?
It is late. Summer hangs heavy in the trees,
And this place, this time, wields invisible stars.

We have all wandered and been sometime lost
In the dear certitudes of our persuasions.
The night wind seemed to speak to us alone.
The arms of those we loved held us close,
And the swift dark of winter seemed a peace.
They came to greet us at the sweeping door,
Snow falling, and have gone where we may not follow,
Full of forgiveness for what we still believed.

Walking the Shore Thinking of Su-Shih

I, too, would like another name,
one mine alone, original sounds
familiar as slow water on sand
in a place where small shore-birds
think nothing of their eloquent tracks
erased, lost ideograms, explanations.

Mountains make me uncomfortable.
They remind me, now, of banishment,
the distant crying of apes
and the struggle of grass among rocks
heaved up into mist.
The cold embarrasses the soul.

It did not for him. How amiable
he seems, nine centuries old
and bringing in a few greens at dusk,
knowing the poem would take place.
When he rose, brushed it on the wall
of his straw hut, it was the mountain's poem.

He did not think of Wang-an Shih
who would have admired the cold,
brilliance of the snow and emptiness,
more serene with every grass-black stroke.

He became his bruised hand, his hand
the poor brush, his brush a civilization.

Bowed salt-grass writes me down
in tufted hummocks. The sea swarms
its flat, gray-blue laid low by the wind,
an unbelonging wind, yet music.
This would not have troubled him,
this idiocy of a long visionary shore.

Wally in the Park

I: April 1953

Now he knew where it might come from,
And said it over to his soft, clasped hands,
"We have made too much of life."

Spring would still arrive, a green haze
Shake in the haw trees along the river.
The snow would vanish unconfessed.

Again and again, another end ending,
As though forgiving its one attempt,
A new proclamation whistled from the trees.

Those voices were familiar, the swift comfort
Of warblers pausing, going north
Into the vast expanse of their small lives.

Far in that million miles of pines
And windy meadows, the purity of waiting
Tempted the white sun with a great emptiness.

It was, he thought, only what he held
In darkness in his hands. He felt it ache,
Fluttering there, eager to be gone.

Patient, he did not let go. The warmth,
A truth, concealing the world from itself,
Was almost the promise he had hoped to find.

He gazed up beyond the trees. The river
Sighed against its banks. One loose cloud
Kept wisping away high up in the blue.

II: Poesis, Eheu Poesis!

He was willing to admit there might just be
Another true poet out there somewhere
In the tall cities or the mountains of Utah.

Sitting on a park bench in the cool sun,
Relieved that winter was over at last,
He leafed through their slim ambitions

Here and there a clear phrase gave him pause,
And shapes rose from lines to be repeated
As he read on looking for fresh intelligence.

It never took long to tell who might come along,
Those for whom a small crack promised a doorway
Through which the chariest guest might enter.

One by one he stacked their offerings beside him.
The wind shuffled in bushes beside the path
Like a mind among many selves, many words.

When he looked up, the white sun made him wince.
He thought of his masters, their hollow voices
Sustaining his way of saying what he knew.

And then he thought of that, of how they'd known
The tissue they inhabited lying there
In the morning darkness, half-dreaming, half-awake.

For them the sun would break among tall trees,
The silver streak across the hills and the day
Scatter about the kitchen through white plates.

He did not mind that he'd become one of them,
Yet to be a minor companion of Virgil drifting
In a vanished life seemed hardly recompense.

The seated body was more than any image;
Breath, a cold fire, a risk in the breast,
Was a new simplicity without reflection.

And, chilled, he felt spring the finest summons,
Morning doing its will. Even the bleak sun
In a world without poets seemed more to cherish.

He would, he promised the quiet taunting him,
Write this down. He had no choice. He knew.
He would feel this way when later was all too late.

Willowrun

So long as she was spared the freezing pilgrimage,
scuffing through snow past the plywood shacks
like a frost-rimed sparrow embossed on blue paper,
spared the white grease in the pan, the dead stove,
the thin floor puffing up with every wind,
the precocious renunciation of warmth, of sun
remembering her bones . . . well, perhaps
the reluctant glories and soft ceremonials
at night of marriage would carry her back
into the soft, beating bosom she had denied.

Waiting all day for him to return again,
she thought of love as a beckoning loneliness.
It was like the snow heaped among willows
or the sound of water under the skim of ice
on the creek, its sumptuous, purled enticement.
Even on Sundays when they climbed and slipped
along the banks and among the barren trees,
the fending invitation stirred her breast,
and the crows, clustered voiceless or stretching
a wing high up in the crowns seemed inscribed.

When she wept at noon, huddled on the couch,
the low sun glancing off the snow dazzled
about the ceiling. Through her tears the two-month

Christmas tree shed needles, tickling like rain
on a small girl's playhouse roof where she could lie
watching the great house beyond the rose beds.
The causeless tears of love for the living and dead
glistened in February's crepitation,
its ominous cenotaphs of snow in the woods,
implausible at noon, ancestored of stars.

And that night as she lay beside him, sleepless,
waiting and watching the moonlit snow repeat
silence and hungerless brilliance in the room,
she heard, as in another life, a tree
heavy with white blossoms, patch-boled,
branch-winding, burst through the kitchen door.
It stretched, sprang leaves, shed paper, curling bark
and twisted against the walls, threw down the pictures
he had hung for her, mounded in the frayed chairs
and slewed the frozen coffee-pot from the stove.

When I Came to Cerillos and Mádrid, New Mexico

In Memoriam: Yvor Winters

I

Now is memory, meaning, wanting all in one
    and the still presence that will capture it,
    calm it, give it to you as your own.

Now is the keen, burst savor of an orange
    flooding your mouth and still aflame
    with the sun and the stored god in the tree.

Now is this friend, close once more, on the mend
    after a long absence and harsh words,
    eyes welling, shining like new leaves.

Now is shade beneath the orange tree and a violet's glint
    in an edge of lowliest green, breathing
    the moist, rich, mould-ripe earth.

Now I have not seen but can see anciently
    the gray-green fallows, the river in April
    slow in the small shallows, the bluffs reflected.

Now I am here: sea-summoned. Now there: land-leavened,
    and I cannot leave one thing behind,
    like Raven, a mind gritting in crimson sage.

II

Long clouds flock Eastward,
the bellwether but a summoning:
salve sancta of silences.
The soft Tanuge spring
has begun, rising through its ruins,
not for us, nor for itself
nor for anything we know.

It lies about everywhere
with nothing to accomplish
for those that sang its coming.
Precise and inimitable
on the arching, gray tree
yet a shamble of shades
and haze that interchange,
now filial air, now twig,
and then neither, it is but
a glissando suggesting green.

And where you wander
in escape and affirmation,
stumbling in the coarse, laid grasses,
beneath your feet time silts
through the teeth of the dead,
men, sheep, cattle, ground squirrel
and the raven's ebony beak.

Wearing the clouds, picket-pin,
you become another part
of the fury of emptiness
in motion, particles ablaze
in the grave, dispassionate dance,
invisible yet intensely felt.
What is it to be born
and know this place is mine?

But you, too, are forgotten,
borne away on the feeling
of sandy soil, limp humus,
and of glinting space and color—
grays, mauve-maizes, raw siennas
tinged by the lark's adulation,
the sun-burnished hawk's "Kyrie!"
and the endless withdrawing
of your life into periphery,
yourself an inattentive moment
in the great, placid beckoning.

III

These in the small horizon
of parched grasses, veined stones
search for you, Poet.

Let them come as though
rising out of the stubborn earth,
laced with loam, weed-wound.

They are ours, the weary,
the famished, the wounded.
They shall find you, know you are here.

This is as it should be,
though merely another colloquial life
among tiny herbs and splayed trees.

But the calling of leaves and white pith?
Why are you, this one, here?
What has arranged you to this place?

All your life long
you have been bound this way.
The cottonwoods waited your coming.

The blood-dark river of winter
believed in you. The *Contrayerba*
knew you would stoop to it.

The many hairy stems,
the abominable seeds, sun-steeping,
trained your eye for the cold, lemony sunrise.

Jose heard you in the distance
where your step bruised the *Inmortal,*
and the healing days took seed.

When you did not believe, you believed.
When you were lonely, you were not alone.
When you were filled with love, you were seized.

The dogs rose to your returning,
and the dead quickened, strained in the walls.
Your bed, at night, shed its frayed covers.

"Somehow, it was you," you said, "barren land
awaiting me." And you knew
as your hand knows, curling in sleep.

The sun lifts there, implacable
along your thin shoulders. Leaves thicken.
Numberless, the old ones wake.

IV

Often at night when sleep
has other ends in view,
I live your severe, fair mind,
and then a passionate kind
of remorse carries me deep
into myself like a screw
fleeing its slotted head
down through a body it fled.

Often, too, I admit
I walk as you in grass
laid dry by the parching sun,
green spring and summer undone.
I rehearse images, wait
words that shall come to pass
through me, out and away
beyond time heaping the day.

Yet that is never enough.
You wary me on toward night
and lamplit windows hung
above a dusty road. How long
you'll do me thus, dear grief,
I alone know. It is late
for both of us, Cerillos
dying still or worse.

How would I recognize
when I had come there, friend?
April discovered me
gazing west at sunset,
the mountains, purpled unrest,
hanging half on end
and long clouds piling like a sea
upside-down, and not a sound
but my heart clutching the ground.

No. Never before like this,
unmade and eager to lose
whatever was mine to waste,
my life like a blind past
stumbling hit-or-miss
in a dark, endless bruise—
and yet at peace, at home,
citizen of weed, rock, loam.

Lake Nine

Old age is a fisherman sitting alone
in a rowboat on a placid lake
waiting for a nibble, obeying
the first rule of fishing—patience.
He had rowed out before daybreak.
The air sweet, soft and mild.
(The taste of it! Ah, yes, the taste of it!)

The oars cheeped in the oarlocks
like small, waking birds.
The reeds drifting under the boat
caressed it, shushed it as it moved
slowly by out to deeper water.
The small anchor lay tangled
in its rope in the prow.

His bending and leaning back have
a steady, pleasing adagio rhythm.
He does not look about, for he knows
how far to go, where to string his line
and wait in the still center
of the small, clear, windless lake.

The boat will not drift,
slowed, let loose, sleeps on the mirror.

He readies his thin pole,
careful to make not a sound,
strings the line, weights it, hookless,
baitless and drops it
over the side.

Sister Theophila at Fond du Lac

The winter was long, colder than ever.
Now the sapphire dragonflies
hover over the small pool
in the hospital garden, dip
and dart and sway for me.

I understand them better,
believe what they pray,
for pray they do. You can
hardly hear it. Listen
with me. It is a small
prayer, a summer prayer
and only here like the sun.

I did not notice this yesterday
listening to my beads,
the years repeating
one sound alone and
the mute companioning.

Trying is shame and remorse
without end, to wear winter
like a cowl, to carry black,
and sit on a swing
in the garden between

heaven and earth,
back and forth, back
and forth, annoyed
by fruit flies, trying on
sapphire.

Galisteo, New Mexico

Easter morning, they go out early,
Cross the swirling Galisteo on a log,
Teetering, vivid in the cold, lemony light,
And, straggling, they climb to an ancient place
Filled with the eyes of seed and failing stone.

Then among the heaved rocks of the crest,
He settles down, wedged, and watches the clouds,
And, far below, the brown river turning its silence
Against the steep, soft banks. Far beyond thought,
He imagined himself there waiting for something.
He saw, at a great distance, a patch of colors,
Pale blue and troubled grays, that had not been there
The morning before. It was not part of the butte.
It was a man sitting without purpose, composed,
A quick, casual stroke in another landscape.

Whatever sense made in that moment swept
Itself away perfecting. The rocks were cold.
The micaed grains of ten thousand summers
Clung to his hand, peppered his patient shoes.
Ants. Shards. The gentle scrape of time
Working its way up through narrow trails,
Stone darkened a moment by a passing hand,
And the white smoke of a small fire—all these

Conspired within him, and his heart thundered
Far off and, then, nearer and nearer.

She called him from where she had waited below
At the steep turning up to the leveled pueblo,
A few vague reminders, a few true finds
Piled in small squares and wanting more,
And low, dry grass, and twigs, and meek weeds.
He called back, looked once more to the west
Out beyond the rising blue, and, slipping, sliding,
Picked his way down into the gray eclogue
Of twisted tamarisk trees and here and there
The half-protruding, bleached bones, sun-stoned,
Wind-washed, unsocketed ruminations of cattle.

Later

I, for one, was disappointed, if not angry.
Here was this thatched, slumped shed,
and, nested among a sorry set of animals
on a mound of rotting straw, a small woman,
a rake-of-a-man, a Jew I guessed, and a child—
all in a challenge of light unlike any light,
ten-thousand-thousand lamps aflame
among shimmering golden cymbals and dawns,
striking out, blazoning, beating back the night,
and the incensed air humming, heaving
as though all the flies of Asia had come home.

Believe me, I could hardly see my feet,
much less think that we three had come,
beaten and pulped by wind and brutal sun
so far for this—merely another prophesy,
at best a king in the world of many kings.
Yet, there I kneeled down in the scattered dung,
Balthasar at my side, his black brow glistening,
and, dropping it once, I laid my crown
at her feet, hidden in blue, swept folds.

They say that Angels sang a name there.
They never sang for me in the best of times,
but, then, a minor lord of a minor people,

no matter his devotion, if he learns anything,
comes to realize the emptiness of songs,
the trivial flattery of poets in the blank face
of what lies ahead. Perhaps it is that,
what lies ahead, that Angels know and sing.
Perhaps I heard them there, compelled
by an ass, a mumbling goat, and a white dove
beating among the beams, for they were there
as absolute as I and I the many ministries
that sing their radiant absolutions in the dark.

I know there is an end to every tale,
yet mine has none that anyone remembers.
The going back was hard as the mindless coming,
and even harder, for there was no star, no promise.
Children, standing in a row before their teacher,
may one day sing and resurrect my life,
that trembling spill like water from a rock.
I dream a thousand years, then thousands more,
the stubborn hero, hunkered down in a field
where sheep bustle and leap about him, over-under,
and the clouds tower and redeemers thunder.

An Oxford Winter

Plato's old man, Socrates,
    knew wisdom bitter
as the memory of love
    drunk in the morning.
Yet there was something alive,
    unforgivable,
in it, for love loved itself,
    suffered its body,
no matter how old, and mind
    no matter how numb.

Farewell tonight, my wise friend.
    It is far too cold
for a mind's symposium
    or conversation
with a book, Greece gone mythic,
    Alcibiades,
that beauty dead by logic.
    How shall the body
understand being a mind?
    What can mind do then?

Well, I close the book, turn out
    the light and Jowett

whose sleeps are longer than mine.
My blankets are harsh,
the wool of England, sheep, grass
dusted with small snow.

II.

Three white, one mottled—
Swans on the Cherwell
through University Park,
    pale umbers and grays,
and, ticking in the leafage
    autumn surrendered,
glazing the sallow reed-beds,
    quiet rain falling.

Where now shall we go?
Over the bright cricket-pitch
toward the great black-green cypress,
    there to shelter us,
    there to watch soft rain
Come down, silvering,
kindly sinking each in thought,
    almost memory,
    the refuse of love
that found us, four souls strolling?

Let us go that way,
catch the cold rain, catch mind
in hand, lift it to the lips
    and profess silence
    like mute swans drifting
beyond excitement, serene.

III.

      Flat caps and whippets
in the muddy courtyard. Boots
      and, in the old pub,
brown lights, glass-gleam and small brass
      glitter behind you,
      and the ruddy folk
hover about, biting ale,
and experience declares:

      "Now your life lives you,
and your soul's last night dreamed you
as someone else, lost and strange.
      What are you doing?"
Ah, but I cannot bear it.
We go back across hoar grass,
      over Port Meadow
      where mongrels run free.

IV.

The gray hours drift by:
    icy, deserted streets.
Walk about. No one knows you.
In that comfort, an immense
    distance reconceives
itself as someone you know.

Lean, look down from the bow-bridge.
Shadows ply the swept water.
    In the rank meadow
three horses running, heavy,
    turf thrown, startled birds.

Later, strains diminishing
    among the cellos,
partridge on the snowy wall
    of the sunken yard,
Mufflered skaters on the pond,
    and, hurrying home,
breaking through the swift twilight
    to enter the dark
    in us as they were,
substance and shriven promise,
prodigies of our lost life.

V.

Below Whitnam Clumps
in the false spring light
of February Sunday,
we wander, called out
into the rich, Roman fields
by the one day sun,
the beckoning in our blood.

Way up there, climbers straggle
across the slope face
to the crown, the trees
in their vague striving,
and the misted, tufted blue.

Later than my life,
earlier than failed remorse,
I stand in an old graveyard.
Yew trees scent the air,
the church shut, unparished,
rebuffs the late soul,
the silent Psalter.
Here mossy slates slant and blur
the wonder of namelessness
where pale grass sours, rank,
scrawls illegibly in sleep.

VI.

I touch the blue tree
in the distance by the Thames,
  there at the slow bend
  in the silver cusp
of water that endures thought.

  Watch me and be whole.
Days in abject decaying,
nights speaking revelations—
  these I have constrained
to realize the depth green,
  devouring the sky,
may entertain and yet live.

  This I have made mine
in the solitude I seize
  upon and am not.
Here I have launched myself forth
into the grand eluding
  offered by this day.
Here I am a sapphire tree
  in a distant eye.

VII.

Tell me what you see:
a fluffed, brown bird in the copse,
    a hedgerow, a fallen gate,
    a lane Hardy walked,
a poem in mind and lost.

    Crocus and lily
    in the greasy mud.
Farther, stand down in new green,
Fifteen centuries, grass-hidden
    Dorchester's vallum,
    centurions spent
for this, a hump-backed pasture.

    Black and white cattle
cluster in lines, cloud-like.
Heavy sky, like them lows,
    Rome oblivious.

VIII.

      Trapped in the doorway
the shadow cannot enter,
      falls back, frayed feathers
drooping to the blood-dark floor,
      quills scraping the jamb.

Who is it guards the lintel,
      gray robes falling loose,
open about the veined thighs?
Surely, it's a man whose long
      disobedience
      is a reflection
and warning of such coming.

      Ah, is it not you,
the mind's terrible double,
      whose reality
      embraces the still
      hesitant shadow?

IX.

I cannot stay here
collecting days, nights, estranged,
    shut up in one room
and writing letters, listening
to *Kindertotenlieder.*

It seems a long way away
    from myself that was.
What is a dead tree, a crown
    of twigs, emptiness
resplendent fastened to
    a sandy bottom?
Logged, it might be of some use,
    the pity of it
unremarkable as chairs.

I stand hours at the window
    watching the cold birds
from an unfamiliar height.
    They rise toward me, flared
up from the bright winter grass,
    black, umber or gray,
all triangle, slant and whisp
    hurled about yet blest
reckless English citizens.
    Raptured by their craft,
my branches wait their coming.
I bend to the noon's wet wind
    in a grief unknown.

X.

     The body itself,
not a mist walking the fields
     in the cold morning,
not a shadow thrown across
     the small, weedy pond,
but body itself, waiting—
     wherever it goes
filled with anticipation
     like a man, head cocked,
listening to what he cannot hear,
     a sound in the grass
that has stopped for a moment,
     and then another,
poised there in taut readiness
     to be going on.
The body living its life:
yes, that's what I have in mind.

Dear Tsvetaeva

For Joseph Brodsky

I have searched everywhere,
room after room, Marina,
for your poems, to hear you
out of the dried-up stars, the cocks
crowing against the slumped dacha.

Those painful impossibilities
that found me as though I, too,
stood there stamping, stamping,
waiting for you to come to me
across the trackless, blue,
moon-withered snow, crystal
and tree-snap, the stars flaking.
There, Osip is with me, and Anna.
Our breath rises through accusations
of the brittle, black branches
and turns to spaces, legends,
silences laid in your life.

God! How cold it is,
how unredeemable the gray ashes
and the tremble of honor
piling up, drifted among the stark
wormwood of mistakes.

In recent day, rumors.

It is as though you were saying this.
These sympathies, these eyes,
Efron, the youth whose brows
bent like drooping wings,
and not to love, having loved
as one swept narrowly
into an exquisite abyss.

These are not my words,
Marina, nor words of the angel
that possessed you. They feel
a sword of eternity,
circling, swinging, sinking
from your lips, your greeting,
to waft slowly, to become mute,
indistinguishable in the rust-gray
refuse of ravens and lying there
in the open chronicle of fields.

Walking in Snow at Midnight

This is the dark too conquering to keep,
Stillness spending the slow phosphoric white.
Bayberry, alder, densely shut, like sheep,
Huddle in the lanes, stir in the night.

Here into shadow sifting, one by one
The moments falter toward infinity.
The soft snow deepens. Presence, overrun,
Trembles to own a white inconstancy.

And measure wanes—still ticking in curled mind,
It could not be insanity or fear,
Never to halt, no matter how unkind,
And never sound, no matter that you hear.

These separated sounds of snow blown down
From burdened trees that ring each trackless field
Are fragile as the drifting in the town
Where, gathered for their rest, the sleepers yield.

And on the sea large snow is nothing sown,
As here, in auraed lights, among these trees,
Where love is nursed, where fury wakes alone,
Or where one stops, composed in what he sees.

So Why?

so why have i been writing
unimportant poems on flowers?

Zbigniew Herbert

I don't know.
I don't, but I go on,
possessed, remade
by the freaked veins, hardly color,
in the vortex of the blue iris,
and the diving darkness there
carries me where I have not
been before over and over
so that our meeting
in the garden at twilight
under the barren branches
and furred twigs and ravelings
of the February jacaranda
becomes another life,
one able to obscure
my tethered unwillingness
to accept silently
the meanness and stupidity
of the world I help go on
out of love for you
and for myself
and for so many others,

known, unknown, present, lost,
half-remembered, perished,
knocking at the door,
who shall also go there,
swung downward into the soft,
the remedial velvet
at the closed pit
of the iris.

Autumn Wind

They will never know, will never live a mind
So fruitfully incomplete, so green MacIntosh.

It was something to think about and almost
Tugged, unpicked, among the satisfied trees.

For a moment, hanging there in the late sun,
He felt the dark promise of roseate pips.

They would seek a downward way, tense as they fell,
And the winesap world melt, ferment for bees.

The sharp winds of autumn and restless snow
Would come upon him. They would not notice.

Thirty miles away in bins at the roadside
The best apples were piled. They were beautiful.

He saw them as he had never seen them before:
Russet, small, firm in hand, Baldwin, Ben Davis.

He lugged from the strand their root-bare ancestors,
Varieties Cato had listed for Caesar's plantation.

Now Snow Apple, Jonathan, Northern Spy, Wealthy
Came here blushing, ten thousand white maidens.

They blessed his lips like winds filled only with snow,
The steady unsolving, tongued end of a thought.

Yes,

there are times when I
could give it all away.
The plum blossoms drift down
on me, lie in my hair,
cling to my arms lovingly.

We have been here together
many years before.
Your ten thousand centers
standing, whiskering sun,
the first soft thrust
of your mauve-bronze leaves eager
to get this all over.

When I came it meant
nothing to you
that I loved being with you,
that I would have embraced you
if I could.

Is it not unbecoming
that I should be in love with you,
a trembling cloud of half-pinks
and half-whites, undecided
about tomorrow?

Surely, I should know better
than to stand here
expecting to be young as you
and wise as spring.

Afterword

I knew Lee Gerlach first as a teacher. My second term in college I landed by chance in his section of an introductory course on modern literature. Every term for the next three years I took every course he offered. The range of the courses may give the impression that I have made them up: Chaucer, pre-twentieth-century American poetry (Edward Taylor and Frederick Goddard Tuckerman were his favorites, but his talks—he didn't lecture—on Emerson were especially sympathetic), twentieth-century American poetry (he had us read dozens of poets arranged like leaves on a big family tree he devised), modern criticism (he was hard on Eliot, and his loyalty to Yvor Winters, his beloved teacher, proved a mixed blessing), and modern European poetry and fiction. He even risked classes on Asian poetry (T'ang and S'ung masters, Persian and Urdu ghazalists, Basho and Issa) and prose (Kawabata, Tanizaki, Narayan, Anand). Day after day I felt he was pouring his plentiful life straight into mine. His voice in reading poems aloud was a beautiful instrument, a manly, measuring tenor, sensitive to the music of the lines, but undramatic, unprofessorial, always keeping a respectful distance from interpretation. It was a revelation of the spiritual radiance of poetry. Even now, thirty years later, I can still hear his voice in my head.

That voice, more meditative, imagistic, and intimate, of course, than the one I heard in class, but no less learned and informing, is the voice that the reader of this book has now had the pleasure of hearing. Gerlach, who is eighty-five, has been writing poems for so long that he has mastered several metrical modes (traditional English verse, syllabic verse, varieties of free verse), worked through several language strata and strategies for configuring the relation of image and statement, and, needless to say, set down the manifold interests, attitudes, and convictions of a long life. Still, the voice in all these poems is recognizably one voice.

"In the Nightstruck House" may well be the earliest poem in the book, a poem written, I suspect, when Gerlach was a member of Winters's school of young poets in the 1950s. Firmly iambic, insistently monosyllabic, the sentences as simple as the rhymes that end them—the poem may seem no more than a period piece, though a fine one. What makes it more than that is the portrait it gives, tender and almost melancholic, of a domestic interior. The man in the poem, a father alone in his house at night, feeling the force of his attachment to his infant son and, at the same time, a nameless, countervailing, and finally undermining force in the very air he breathes, is a figure one finds in many of Gerlach's poems. "White Nights in Mission Hills," a suite of three poems, two set in the poet's house on the rim of a wooded canyon in San Diego, is perhaps the best of these. Solitary, in need of solitude, but looking back at what he has strayed from, Gerlach's householder is surely one of the representative figures in American poetry since World War II. Gerlach's handling of blank verse in this suite, his susceptibility to wonderment and joy, and, most of all, his evocative descriptions of the natural world and his responsiveness to it, its beauty and otherness, its allurements. "The greatest poverty is not to live / In a physical world," I heard him quote in class. Few American poets have lived so richly in that world. Still, unlike poets who fill up lines with notations of phenomena, mere statistics of attention, Gerlach seeks always to understand his experience of the world he knows and loves well. At times he does so memorably, as here:

Reality will keep

blossoming, take leaf,
no matter how
we rest or go.

And here:

> Dry country.
> Surrounded by city, this archaic place resists
> Tomorrow. The owl hunts here. Kit fox and possum
> And skunk clamber through cover up to the lawns.
> Children of moonwalkers watch from the dark door.
> Here they come, shadows emerging from black ice,
> Old fleece, a blur, a soft bristle sliding.
> Hesitant, they gather at the edge of the clipped yard,
> Stand there, alert and ancestral, waiting to speak

These lines, like a modern poetic Lascaux, have haunted me for twenty-five years.

I was delighted to discover in these pages a poem, "In spring flowers, such as those described," I hadn't read before. It seems to me an extraordinary poem, Gerlach's writing at its most characteristic and beautiful. From the opening line, which might have been lifted from some field guide to North American wildflowers, the poem moves through a series of associations, from the field guide note to an image of pistils as violin bows, to memories of a childhood in Wisconsin, that "left-handed mitten," to the historical memory of the Native Americans, Chippewa and Fox and Sac, who dwelled in the poet's woods, making music, too, before the poet was. Connecting it all—flowers, music, woods, humans—is grass, earth's complex and beneficent universal:

> Wherever you go—the grass family, slender
> And tall with hollow, round stems, spikelets, scales.
>
> There the triticum ripen, the inner and outer sleaves,
> Feathery stigmas savour the sun and are grain.

The poem may remind the reader of Whitman's "A child said *What is the grass?*" But Gerlach's poem takes a closer, not to say more scholarly, look at things than Whitman's, its images are both more exact and arrestingly strange, and Gerlach's soul-surrender, in memory and in meditation as he writes, is more personal and, to my mind, more persuasive because less speculative, than Whitman's:

> I have gazed into the bristly crowfoot, its hairs
> Spreading like the sun, and forgotten the way back.
>
> I have walked these woods, have sucked the grass.
> I have listened to the oaks, the andantes of waterleaf.

Reading these lines—this poem—requires attention, but it is attention the reader gives necessarily and almost unwittingly. Pleasure gives way to absorption, and then for a while there is only the poem.

This book is just the second of Gerlach's not privately printed. His first, *Highwater*, came out only three years ago. For too many years I was afraid that he was destined to join that group of American poets who remained all but unknown while alive because they were unpublished or published too little—Taylor, Jones Very, Tuckerman, Emily Dickinson, Trumbull Stickney, Weldon Kees, Henri Coulette, Dick Barnes, and others. We owe a debt of gratitude to Swallow Press / Ohio University Press for making it more possible for Gerlach to win his readers now.

Harry Thomas